SOME LIMERICKS

SOME LIMERICKS

Collected for the use of Students,
& ensplendour'd with Introduction,
Geographical Index, and with Notes
Explanatory and Critical

BY

NORMAN DOUGLAS

GROVE PRESS, INC.
NEW YORK

TO
THE UNKNOWN POET

CONTENTS

INTRODUCTION

He must be a quintessential fool who does not realize that the following fifty limericks are a document of enduring value. And I beg leave to say that the collection has been made not for such people, but for those who can appreciate its significance.

I may be abused on the ground that the pieces are coarse, obscene, and so forth. Why, so they are; and whoever suffers from that trying form of degeneracy which is horrified at coarseness had better close the book at once and send it back to me, in the hope that I may be simple enough to refund him the money. As to abuse—I thrive on it. Abuse, hearty abuse, is a tonic to all save men of indifferent health. At the same time I am fully convinced that nobody under the age of ten should peruse these pages, since he would find them so obscure in places that he might be discouraged from taking up the subject later on, which would be a pity. Ten, and not before, is the right age to commence similar studies; a boy of ten is as sagacious and profound as one of eighteen, and often more intellectual. Ten was the precise age (see page 35) at which I began to take interest in this class of literature, and it has done me all the good in the world.

There was a time when one collected butterflies, or flowers, or minerals. But the choicest specimen of (say) precious opal can be replaced, if lost. Now if these limericks are lost, they cannot be replaced; they are gone for good. You may invent new ones, as many as you please. Such new ones, however, will inevitably have another tone, another aroma, because they belong to another age. The discerning critic will detect a gulf both in technique and in feeling between most of the limericks of the Golden Period and those of today, and naturally enough, seeing that the poets, and not only the poets of the Victorian and the Georgian epochs have an entirely different outlook. Precious opal remains the same yesterday, today, and fifty thousand years hence.

That is why lately, with increasing intelligence, I have taken to garnering what future collectors cannot hope to possess without my aid—perishable material such as the Street Games of London children, or the blasphemies of Florentine coachmen. It would interest me to know what proportion of those thousand-odd Street Games are still played, and which of them have died out in the short interval since my little book on the subject was written. In that book itself I predict their decline, and give reasons for it (page 119–121). And it is the same with the swear words. I caught the old ones in the nick of time. A good half of them have already grown obsolete and are unfamiliar to the new generation of such men. Why is this? Because these men, being no longer cab-drivers but chauffeurs, are afflicted with the neurasthenia common to all such mechanical folk; they lack—their distemper makes them imagine they lack—the leisure which is essential to the creation of original works of art, however humble; they forget the ripe old blasphemies and have not the wit to invent a fresh supply. How shall good things be generated if, instead of sitting over your wine and cheese, you gulp down a thimbleful of black coffee and rush off again? Mechanics, not microbes, are the menace to civilization.

A writer in the *New Witness* (Dec. 9, 1921) once suggested that this collection of swear words should be privately printed. That cannot be done; it will never see the light of day. But I shall now permit myself, for

reasons which will be apparent later on, to reproduce
the few words of introduction which I wrote for it in
the year 1917:

"Nor is there much bad language to be found in
Romola. Perhaps the Florentines did not swear so
horribly in those days. Perhaps their present fondness
for impious invective is likewise a reaction from Savonarola's teaching (I had been discussing Savonarola's
puritanism). For Tuscans of today are pretty good
blasphemers. They have many oaths in common but,
unlike others, they pride themselves upon an individual
tone in this department. A self-respecting Florentine
would consider his life ill-spent had he not tried to add
at least one blasphemy of his own personal composition
to the city stock; it survives, or not, according to its
merits. Of how many other art-products can it be said
that merit, and merit alone, decides their survival?

"Adventures are to be adventurous.

"I have begun to make a collection of these curses,
imprecations, objurgations—abusive, vituperative or blas-
phemous expletives: swear words, in short. It already
numbers thirty-eight specimens, all authentic, to the best
of my knowledge. Most of them, I regret to say, are
coupled with the name of the Deity. That cannot be
helped. I propose to treat the subject in a scientific spirit
—from the "kulturhistorischen Standpunkt", as the
Germans say. I did not invent the swear words, and if
the reader dislikes their tone he may blame not me but
Savonarola for generating this pungent reaction from his
bigotry. Violence always begets violence.

"Why not interest oneself in such things? Man cannot
live without a hobby. And this is folklore, neither more
nor less; an honorable hobby. Furthermore, unlike stamp
or coin collecting, it costs practically nothing; a season-

13

able one. It has the additional advantage that the field is virgin soil and the supply of material very considerable —unlimited, I should say. Moreover, the research leads you into strange byways of thought and causes you to ponder deeply concerning human nature; some of these oaths require a deal of explanation; a philosopher's hobby! Unexploited, unexplained, unexhaustible—what more can be asked? And, as aforesaid, absurdly economical.

"There is yet more to be said in its favour. For while these swear words are as genuine a flower of the soil as Dante or Donatello and every bit as characteristic, they happen to be up to date. A live hobby! They portray modern Tuscany with greater truthfulness than any other local product. Indeed, it will not take you long to discover that they, and they alone, are still flourishing in this city. For the rest of Florence is dead or dying. The town decays, declines; it shrinks into a village; grows more provincial every day. Political life has yielded up the ghost; art and literature and science, music and the state—they gasp for breath. There is no onward movement perceptible. It either stands still, or moves actually backwards. The oaths alone are vital. In lightning flashes, and with terrible candour, they reveal the *genius loci*."

Are not these words, most of them, applicable to a collection of English limericks? A curious parallel! "A self-respecting Englishman would consider his life ill-spent had he not tried to add at least one limerick of his own personal composition to the national stock; it survives, or not, according to its merits"—how true!

And what shall we write instead of *Savonarola?* We can write *puritanism;* indeed, we must. This verse-form is a belated product of puritanical repression. That is why Latin races cannot appreciate such literature. If you tell a Frenchman:

> Il y avait un jeune homme de Dijon,
> Qui n'avait que peu de religion.
>> Il dit: "Quant à moi,
>> Je déteste tous les trois,
> Le Père, et le Fils, et le Pigeon"—

he will look at you in a dazed fashion, wondering whether he has heard aright, while Spaniards are positively shocked when you translate for them a lyric such as:

> There was a young girl of Spitzbergen,
> Whose people all thought her a virgin,
>> Till they found her in bed,
>> With her quim very red,
> And the head of a kid just emergin'.

They regard these things as dirty. Now tell them that all such "dirt" is the outcome of protestant theories of life, and that the poets of the Restoration expressed the same reactionary spirit in other metres, and they will suggest that you become a convert to the R. C. Faith which, they declare, is based on notions that are both cleaner and saner. "We don't require such ambiguous outlets," they say. It may be true. They may not require them. But they need them. For what have they not lost, these Latins, with their Catholicism! One limerick is worth all the musty old Saints in their Calendar. Saints are dead—they have died out from sheer inability to propagate their species; limericks are alive, and their procreative capacity is amazing. (One would like to know how many new ones are born every day.) The cult of Saints is mediaeval affectation; the cult of limericks, as I shall presently show, is a Bond of Empire.

No doubt malnutrition plays a part, and Southern races are apt to be underfed. Limericks are jovial things. An empty stomach is hostile to every form of joviality; it can produce nothing like the generous and full-blooded lines already quoted. Our own half-starved classes are a case in point: they know not these poems. The well-fed youngsters of the universities and the stock exchange, commercial travellers for good houses, together with a wise old scholar or two—these are the fountainheads. It is gratifying, meanwhile, to have captured a few specimens of what, historically speaking, is a protest against protestantism, and strange to think that our little ones would never have learnt to babble about the "old man of Kent, whose tool was remarkably bent," or "the young man of Fife, who couldn't get into his wife," but for Luther's preaching and the victories of Naseby and Dunbar.

Whatever may be thought of speculations such as these, there is no denying that limericks are a yea-saying to life in a world that has grown grey. That alone justifies their existence. They are also English—English to the core. Of how many things can that be said? Take only our other poets: can it be said that Milton, or Keats, are English? They may have been born in England, and they certainly write the language of that country—quite readable stuff, some of it. But how full of classical allusions, what a surfeit of airs and graces! Open their pages where you will, and you find them permeated by a cloying academic flavour; one would think they were written for the delectation of college professors. The bodies of these men were English, but their souls lived abroad; and the worst of it is, they carry their readers' souls abroad with them—abroad, into old Greece and God knows where, into the company of Virgil and Ariosto and Plato and other foreigners.

There is none of that continental nonsense here. Limericks are as English as roast beef; they, and they alone, possess that harmonious homely ring which warms our hearts when we hear them repeated round the camp-fire. Wherever two or three of our countrymen are gathered together in rough parts of the world, there you will find these verses; it is limericks that keep the flag flying, that fill you with a breath of old England in strange lands, and constitute one of the strongest senti-mental links binding our Colonies to the mother-country. Indeed, I should say that their political value is hardly appreciated at home, and that the Colonial Office might do worse than install a special department for the pro-duction and export of ever-fresh material of this kind (I have reason to think that such a department is already in existence). These planters and Civil servants, the cream of our youth, might often suffer from the irritation pro-duced by living lonely lives in lonely places; they might often be at loggerheads with each other, but for the healing and convivial influence of limericks that remind them of common ties and common duties and a common ancestry, and make them forget their separate little troubles. Or do you fancy they discuss art and politics in their leisure moments? If so, you have never lived among them. Can you hear one of them reciting cosmopolitan effusions like the Ode to a Nightingale or Paradise Re-gained? Let him try it on!

When we consider the popularity of limericks wherever our tongue is spoken, it is surprising how few of them can be traced to a definite author. In no other branch of literature do we find so great a number of anonymous writers, writers of talent and industry, sometimes of genius, whose labours have received no adequate reward or even acknowledgment. We hear of the Unknown Soldier: what of the Unknown Poet? Is he never to have his memorial? I have done my little best in dedicating to him the following pages. Another appropriate inscription would have been to Queen Victoria, under whose reign these verses achieved their highest development. Edward Lear has been fruitful and suggestive. Yet it is open to doubt whether he was the actual inventor of such poems, as Professor Saintsbury (*History of Prosody*, III, p. 389, note) seems to imply; the verse must have existed before his time, but he popularised it and fixed the epigrammatic form. We have now abandoned his tiresome canon by which the last word of the last line is identical with the last word of the first; the chief difference, however, is that ours have a deliberate meaning, while his are deliberate nonsense.

Limericks alone would have made the Victorian epoch memorable. That was the Golden Period. We are now in the Silver Age, the sophisticated age, the age of laborious ornamentation, such as:

There was a young girl of Aberystwith,
Who went to the mill they grind grist with, etc.

or

There were three young ladies of Grimsby,
Who asked: "Of what use can our quims be," etc.

or

There was a young girl of Antigua,
Whose mother said: "How very big you are," etc.

or (a less familiar example of this exotic school)

There was an old man at the Terminus,
Whose bush and whose bum were all verminous.
    They said: "You *sale Boche!*
    You really must wash
Before you start planting your sperm in us."

Some of these baroque things are not without charm, but one gladly returns to the Aeschylean simplicity of the earlier period.

I said that limericks were English; I should have said, English and American. Whatever one may think of America's achievements in other fields, it must be admitted that in this one she is a worthy competitor with the old country and that her productions are all that could be desired in point of structural excellence and delicacy of imagination.

Not for nothing did the Mayflower sail westwards. And thank Heaven the cabin-passengers were puritans and not catholics! If, later on, these good people indulged in a little amateurish witch-burning out there, they have now made amends by the non-amateurish quality of their limericks. This verse-form, as we all know, is of yesterday, but, once imported into the New World, it struck its deepest roots into the soil most congenial to such a growth—the soil of the Eastern States. The New England regions are by far the most productive, and such examples as are here given have been garnered one and all by an assiduous lady-collector of Boston in the immediate vicinity of her home. Though dealing with different parts of America and of the world they are without exception a local product; so she assures me. I am sorry to have been able to include only a few samples from her richly varied store; sorrier still not to be able to thank her in this place for her kindness in allowing me the use of these specimens. She has made it a condition that her name shall not be mentioned in connexion with them.

And this would bring me to the final and pleasant task of acknowledging my debt to a number of other contributors, mostly of a still youthful age. I find myself, however, in a serious dilemma; none of them—no, not a single one—will permit me to print his or her name. Never did I have so many ardent collaborators, and never such modest ones! Their unanimity in the matter is both rare and praiseworthy, and yet I must be allowed to say that even such a commendable trait as self-effacement can be pushed too far, when it leaves another man in the awkward position of being unable to perform what he considers his duty. Modesty is no doubt a charming characteristic of youth, but I never knew what that word really meant, till I embarked on this little undertaking.

LIMERICKS

There was a young plumber of Leigh,
Who was plumbing a girl by the sea.
    Said she: "Stop your plumbing:
    There's somebody coming!"
Said the plumber, still plumbing: "It's me."

Variant:

    When she said: "Some one's coming!"
    He answered (still plumbing):
"If any one's coming, it's me."

The temptation of printing this favourite is not to be resisted, although every man, woman and child in England knows it by heart just now.

Will they know it in fifty years' time?

That is my point.

I do not wish to appear captious but, having lived there, I should like to observe that the place is called Leigh-on-Sea only by courtesy. It is not on the sea; it is on the estuary of the Thames. And when the tide is out you see neither rock nor shingle nor sand, but an expanse of oozy mudflats intersected by tidal creeks. These mudflats, with the sunlight on them, are to my eyes the chief beauty of Leigh; they glitter, or rather shine, like liquid gold. Picturesque, abundantly; but quite unfitted for plumbing purposes. Think of the girl's dress!

23

There was an old girl from Kilkenny,
Whose usual charge was a penny.
For the half of the sum
You might roger her bum —
A source of amusement to many.

Golden Period: an improvement on Lear's version.

Kilkenny, a slumbrous old town famed for its cats and monastic ruins, is not the kind of place to harbour people of this profession. Puzzling over the matter, and scrutinizing the text more closely, I find that the lady is described not as *of* Kilkenny but as *from* there. I conclude, accordingly, that in youth she found her way from the green fields of Leinster into some Dublin establishment, like many another country girl; and that it is her activities in the capital which are here commemorated.

Be that as it may, nobody can complain of her charges.

That naughty old Sappho of Greece
Said: "What I prefer to a piece
    Is to have my pudenda
    Rubbed hard by the enda
The little pink nose of my niece."

American.

These lines being unintelligible to me, I sent them to my lady-specialist for comment and elucidation. Her reply, I confess, leaves me where I was—in complete ignorance of what the poem is about. She writes: "I learnt no Greek at school, but have of course heard of Sappho's poems. They must be fifth-rate stuff, if she knew no more about poetry than she did about other things. The nose: what next? Be sure, dear Sir, there is some mistake here. The suggestion is too absurd. No woman is ever so much of a fool, not even under the influence of drink."

I will leave it there, and wait for enlightenment from some other quarter, merely noting that Sappho was not born in Greece (though a good many other people were) and that tradition fails to record whether she had a niece or not.

There were two young men of Cawnpore,
Who buggared and fucked the same whore.
    But the partition split,
    And the spunk and the shit
Rolled out in great lumps on the floor.

Rather coarse, the last two lines; they have a school-boy flavour.

The danger of this playful practice was shown up some years ago in Tunis papers, which reported how two Arabs were sentenced in the local Court for behaving in a similar fashion to a young native girl.

Cawnpore, famous for the massacre of Europeans in 1857, is—to the best of my recollection—an uncommonly dull place; duller even than Lucknow. I see no reason why young people should not try to amuse themselves as best they can, in such a hole. At the same time, it would have been wise if one or the other of them had controlled his impatience and waited his turn. And what was the lady doing, to allow this proceeding: Being a prostitute, she ought to have known what she was about. Such blame, therefore, as attaches to her should not be withheld.

There was a young girl of Pitlochry,
Who was had by a man in a rockery.
    She said: "Oh! You've come
    All over my bum;
This isn't a fuck — it's a mockery."

There are several fine country seats near Pitlochry and a good many of them may have rockeries in their grounds, but the text, as it stands, does not allow us to decide in which of them this event took place.

To make it intelligible, we must suppose that it took place during a dance; at night, therefore, when one gropes about and is less sure of one's position than by daytime. We must remember, too, that it happened in a rockery, whose uneven surface is not conducive to successful copulation. The fiasco may not have been the man's fault altogether, though the lady's resentment is perfectly justifiable.

They will know better next time. They will realize that rockeries are built for ferns and not for fucks.

There was a young fellow called Grant,
Who was made like the Sensitive Plant.
When asked: "Do you fuck?"
He replied: "No such luck!
I would if I could, but I can't."

The beauty of these lines recalls the Golden Period. They are quite modern.

The Plant hymned by Shelley was psychologically sensitive:

But none ever trembled and panted with bliss
In the garden, the field, or the wilderness,
Like a doe in the noontide with love's sweet want,
As the companionless Sensitive Plant.

If our poet had this variety of Plant in mind, it would signify nothing more than that the young man was "companionless," or chaste, or shy, to an abnormal degree. He might end in overcoming this defect with the help of some good woman, especially if he refrains from certain practices to which he is doubtless addicted.

I am inclined to think, however, that the reference is to the true mimosa which is physiologically sensitive, and of which Erasmus Darwin writes:

Weak with nice sense the chaste mimosa stands,
From each rude touch withdraws her timid hands.

And so it is. When you come across a patch of them, you have only to touch a single one with the tip of your finger—down they all go! A pretty sight in the case of a plant, but not in that of a man. This drooping-on-contact mischief is organic, incurable. I see no help for the poor devil, since the ministrations of good women tend only to aggravate a complaint which, fortunately, is not shared by all of us.

"I would if I could, but I can't": there is pathos in that line.

There was a young girl of Samoa,
Who determined that no one should know her.
　　One young fellow tried,
　　But she wriggled aside,
And spilled all the spermatozoa.

Samoa, famous for the rivalry between King Ma-
taafa and King Malietoa, the latter of whom was favoured by the British Government—Samoa, I say, is just
the sort of place where such things should *not* occur, and
"Going Native" has very kindly supplied me with the
following note:

"He must have been an amateur, a European. The
corporal juxta-position is not quite clear to me, but he
seems to have tried topside on, which is difficult with any
one who is both muscular and unwilling, unless you are
prepared to strangle them into unconsciousness first—
and that, believe me! is risky, as you are so liable to
overdo the trick. I don't know about Samoa, but in our
Group a scientific rape always begins sideways on and
face to face (ends according to fancy). When people,
even strong ones, are on their sides, the upper leg can
easily be pushed away from the lower, and if, simulta-
neously, you interpose your body, allowing its weight to
rest upon the lower leg, which must then gradually be
worked behind your back, there is no more 'wriggling
aside'; it is merely a question of gentlemanly perseverance."

Samoan papers please copy.

There was an old fellow of Brest,
Who sucked off his wife with a zest.
    Despite her great yowls
    He sucked out her bowels,
And spat them all over her chest.

A French practice, though not confined to France;
here we have a confirmation of its dangers. One is glad to
know that the lady was his own wife, and not anybody
else's.

Connubial love can take other forms as well:

There was an old man of Dundee,
Who came home as drunk as could be.
    He wound up the clock
    With the end of his cock,
And buggared his wife with the key.

I have been assured that the first of these two ex-
quisite lyrics is by Tennyson; that he wrote numbers of
such, and that nearly all were destroyed after his death.
In point of finish and good taste it is quite worthy of him,
and that he should have indulged his genius with this
class of poetry does not strike me as very unlikely. Whoever perpetrates solemn rubbish like the *Idyls* must feel
the need of unburdening himself from time to time,
especially when gifted with his powers of versification.
Indeed, I should say that whoever lives Tennyson's life
must write an occasional limerick, or burst; and it would
not surprise me to learn, when the real truth about him
is published, that he died "with a limerick on his lips."

There was a young lady of Thun,
Who was blocked by the Man in the Moon.
"Well, it has been great fun,"
She remarked when he'd done,
"But I'm sorry you came quite so soon."

Better things might have been expected of an old
bird like the Man in the Moon whose lady-love, in the
last line, voices the universal grievance of all civilized
women.

We often say that our girls should learn this and
that, and be brought up to "our" standard, but it strikes
me that, in sexual matters, the male would also be none
the worse for some elementary education. An Arab child
called Cheira once lamented to me that, much as she
liked the European's money, she abhorred his bedside
manners; "they come and go like dogs," she declared. It
is not giving our girls a chance, to treat them in this
happy-go-lucky fashion, and I should be interested to discover what proportion of unsatisfactory marriages are
due to the bare fact that the male partner does not know
his business. The copulatory art has to be learnt, like
every other one, unless we want to remain on the level
of the beast.

Let us hope that some authority like Dr. Marie
Stopes will expatiate on this great wrong done to her
sex, and propose a fitting remedy.

There was a young man of Nantucket,
Whose prick was so long he could suck it.
    He said, with a grin,
As he wiped off his chin:
"If my ear were a cunt I could fuck it."

It is fortunate that this particular gift should be confined to a few favoured individuals, or some of us would be doing nothing else all day long.

"If my ear, etc." If! Always that "if"! If his mother were a motor-bus, she would doubtless be provided with wheels.

A charming description of the old port of Nantucket will be found in *Moby Dick* by Herman Melville, who fails, however—though he mentions the whale-fisheries—to note one of the most remarkable things that ever happened there:

There was an old girl of Nantucket,
Who went down to hell in a bucket.
    When asked to come out,
    She replied, with a shout:
"Arse-holes, you buggars! And suck it."

An adventurous but rather rude old lady . . . .

Another unusual male accomplishment is recorded in these lines:

There was an old man who could piss
Through a ring — and, what's more, never miss.
    People came by the score
    And bellowed: "Encore!
Won't you do it again, Sir? Bis! Bis!"

That the performer should have been an old man is highly creditable to him. Young people, as a rule, are far more proficient at this game.

There was a young man of Peru
Who was hard up for something to do.
So he took out his carrot,
And buggared his parrot,
And sent the results to the Zoo.

Golden Period.
It is always when people are idle or "tired of doing nothing," as they call it, that these things occur. Which of us has not been told that:

There was a young monk of Siberia,
Who of frigging grew weary and wearier.
At last, with a yell,
He burst from his cell,
And buggared the Father Superior.

Half the cases of rape recorded in the newspapers, the epidemics of onanism among schoolboys—to say nothing of a great many murders—would never be heard of, if the perpetrators were not *hard up for something to do.* The larger apes in captivity, notably mandrills, are liable to masturbate themselves into a consumption from sheer boredom, and it is not difficult to guess what would happen in such circumstances, if there were a bird handy. So true are the words of Dr. Watts:

Satan finds some mischief still
For idle hands to do.

According to C. E. Hillier (*Avifauna of the Peru-*

vian Highlands, London, 1888, p. 163) Peruvian parrots are of an "unusually confiding disposition." This may supply a key.

He *sent the results to the Zoo*—where, it is to be feared, so delicate a hybrid cannot have survived for long. I conjecture the specimen is now in the Museum of the College of Surgeons.

There was a young man of Belgravia,
Who cared neither for God nor his Saviour.
    He walked down the Strand
    With his balls in his hand,
And was had up for indecent behaviour.

This is the first limerick I ever learnt, at the age of
ten; it has remained fixed in my memory. How many
other things have been forgotten! I print it chiefly to
show that even at this early period our absurd London
street-regulations were already in force. Are they never
going to be repealed?

Belgravia in those days was a fashionable quarter,
in contradistinction to the neighbouring Pimlico, though
an equal amount of copulation went on in both of them.
Yet the Pimlico standard was unquestionably lower:

There was a young lady of Slough,
Who said that she didn't know how.
    Then a young fellow caught her,
    And jolly well taught her —
She lodges in Pimlico now.

And so do a good many others of her kind.

There was a young Royal Marine,
Who tried to fart "God save the Queen."
　　When he reached the soprano
　　Out came the guano,
And his breeches weren't fit to be seen.

"God save the Queen": that gives the approximate date of this gem.

The soprano begins with the stirring words "Send her victorious," and the muscular strain involved in producing these high notes may have led to the disaster. A fit of coughing, or even laughter, has been known to result in a similar cataclysm—a distressing state of affairs, if you happen to be in society at the moment.

The talent of this young Marine, though rare, is not unique. Visitors to the Paris exhibition of 1889, if they frequented certain low haunts, will remember a performer called "l'homme pétard," who achieved wonderful effects on the same organ. His vocal range was amazing, and the soprano notes worthy of Tetrazzini. It has since occurred to me that he may have concealed about his person the musical instrument called "pétophone," a specimen of which I bought in Naples many years ago. It is carried in a trousers' pocket and, when squeezed, imitates that particular *vox humana* so beautifully that, after a hush of general consternation, it becomes a great success at dinner parties, diplomatic receptions, Royal levées, etc.

I should have liked to add a few words on the guano deposits of Peru and of Saint Paul's Rocks, but this note is already too long.

There was a young lady at sea,
Who complained that it hurt her to pee.
    Said the brawny old mate:
    "That accounts for the fate
Of the cook, and the captain, and me."

It is to be hoped that the vessel carried a duly quali-
fied surgeon, else one or the other of the sufferers might
have been in hospital later on. A neglected clap is not all
beer and skittles—beer, indeed, is strictly to be avoided,
and jerky games may send the gonococks lower down
with sad consequences, unless you are wearing a sus-
pender. And even then . . . .

Readers will note the genial conciseness of these
lines. How much truer poetry they are than a great deal
of what is printed under that name!

There was a young man of Newcastle,
Who tied up a shit in a parcel,
    And sent it to Spain
    With a note to explain
That it came from his grandmother's arsell.

Readers will naturally be anxious to learn the contents of this note. I happen to possess a copy. It is addressed to the Spanish Ministry of Agriculture, and runs as follows:

"Sir,

My busniss often takes me to Spanish ports, where I see a deal of waist land round about. I arsked why not manure it? They say, becose weve got no cowse in Spain. I arsked why not use your own shit? They say, becose we don't eat much in Spain, so we can't shit properly. That is why I send you with this post a sample of our Newcastle stuff, it comes from my grandmother who is a hearty old lady free from all teint of desease. Perhaps you will have it anilised and I can supply you with tons of same up to sample strength becose we people, coal-minors though we be, do eat properly and shit properly f.o.b. Newcastle to any Spanish port at reasonable charges and so change your country from a wilderniss into a smiling Paridise and I don't think your people would mind the smell very much once they get used to it.

    Yrs obediently
    . . . ."

There was a young girl of Detroit,
Who at fucking was very adroit.
  She could squeeze her vagina
  To a pin-point and finer,
Or open it out like a quoit.

American.

So far as my experience goes, the faculty which this young lady possessed in so superlative a degree does not come naturally save to a small percentage of women. It has to be learnt; and a good deal, of course, depends on the teacher. Some learn it easily—one might almost say with delight; others succeed only after a certain amount of conscientious experimentation. A considerable number (chiefly southerners) are unteachable, hopelessly unteachable; not a few, again, simply too lazy. To this class belonged a pretty but phlegmatic English girl who once applied to me for the best method of retaining the affection of a gentleman friend. I told her. She said: "Oh, but I can't be bothered like that each time." Soon afterwards I learnt that her friend had discovered somebody else who could, and gladly would, be "bothered."

It follows that women, married or single, have also something to learn (compare page 31).

There was a young mate of a luggar,
Who took out a girl just to hug her.
"I've my monthlies," she said,
"And a cold in the head,
"But my bowels work well . . . do you buggar?"

A forward young minx. I trust he began operations by smacking her little behind with the back of a hairbrush.

It is not likely that either of them will care to reveal what happened after that.

Here is another instance of feminine pertness:

There was a young woman who lay
With her legs wide apart in the hay.
Then, calling a ploughman,
She said: "Do it now, man!
Don't wait till your hair has turned grey!"

And we all know about the young ladies of Birmingham and what they did to a Bishop while he was confirming 'em.

There was a young man of Devizes,
Whose balls were of different sizes.
 One was so small,
  It was nothing at all;
The other took numerous prizes.

Variant:

 His tool, when at ease,
  Reached down to his knees;
Oh, what must it be when it rises.

If one of his testicles was "nothing at all," then this young prize-winner was monorchous. Such people were credited in antiquity with great sexual vigour, and the three or four of them whom it has been my privilege to know certainly corroborated the old belief. But they are up a tree when their single testicle has to be removed by a surgical operation, whereas most of us have a second one in reserve. Even that is doomed to extraction all too frequently!

The fact is, these objects in their present situation are exposed to so many risks that we may well envy the whales, and in a booklet entitled "Hints for God" I make bold to suggest that, at the next creation of the world, they be located in a position of greater security. If He agrees to my proposal He will earn the gratitude of all save a few little boys whose testicles remain hidden upstairs, and are anyhow too small to be taken seriously.

Whoever wishes to see what this organ can do in the way of size should go to Pernambuco, where it is nothing out of the way to see a man wheeling his testicles in front of him on a barrow. I suspect the disease (elephantiasis) was imported by African negroes.

There was a young man of Australia,
Who painted his bum like a dahlia.
    The drawing was fine,
    The colour divine,
The scent — ah! that was a failure.

Flowers can be put to strange uses:

There was an aesthetic young Miss,
Who thought it the apex of bliss
    To jazz herself silly
    With the bud of a lily,
Then go to the garden and piss.

These lines are American, but it is just the kind of thing our own girls used to do in the "Yellow Book" period.

To return to our young Australian—

As no European would behave in this fashion, we must suppose him to have been a native. And since these natives know nothing of paint, it follows that tattooing in colours is intended. Australian tattooing is of no great repute; the practice is certainly less common there than among the New Zealanders, who used to be masters of the art, second only to the Japanese.

Apropos of Japan—readers of Madame Chrysanthème will recall a passage describing how that identical region of the body was ingeniously utilized in the tattooing of a foxhunt.

Dahlias are not indigenous to Australia, but to

Mexico and Central America. The young man, therefore, cannot have set out to portray a flower which was unfamiliar to him; he probably attempted a local plant (his artistic effort is said to have been "*like* a dahlia"), and it was doubtless a spectator, some prying Englishman, who thought to detect a resemblance between a dahlia and the tattooed surface. My botanical expert writes: "Dahlias are first mentioned by Hernandez in his History of Mexico, 1651; later on by the Frenchman Ménonville, who went out there to steal the red cochineal insect from the Spaniards. Named "for" Andrew Dahl, Swedish botanist, and introduced into England by the Marchioness of Bute; afterwards by Lady Holland to Holland House. All dahlias, including the variety *cocksinia,* are scentless."

There was a young man of Natal,
Who was having a Hottentot gal.
 She said: "Oh, you sluggard!"
 He said: "You be buggared!
I like to fuck slow, and I shall."

Here is a manly young fellow who knows what he wants, and means to get it. One would like to shake hands with him.

The words ascribed to the girl are excusable only in the case of a virgin. Otherwise they prove her to be ignorant of the refinements named on page 40 (most savages, indeed, belong to the "unteachable" class). Hottentot women, I am told, are unique among their kind inasmuch as their private parts are covered by a flap of skin which has to be drawn up before coition can take place. I cannot quite visualize this state of affairs, but my informant, an English sea-captain, described it as "great fun."

Another reference to the same district:

There was a young man of Natal,
And Sue was the name of his gal.
 He went out one day
 For a damned long way —
Right up the Suez Canal.

Suez Canal shares are an attractive investment, but the town itself has lost all its former charms. Nothing doing, nowadays, in the donkey line. It is high time the British government took it over again.

47

There was a young man of Bengal,
Who went to a fancy-dress ball.
> Just for a whim
> He dressed up as a quim,
And was had by the dog in the hall.

This must be the same quimsical youngster who, on another such occasion, wore a frill round his tool and went as a ham. Bengal is a lively place, and the ladies are also not coy.

There was a young man of Bengal,
Who swore he had only one ball.
> Then two little bitches,
> They pulled down his breeches,
And found he had none at all.

I witnessed a similar incident long ago in a third-class railway compartment near Manchester, where a handful of factory-girls forcefully undressed a boy amid shrieks of laughter. Although his outfit left nothing to be desired, they did not succeed in making him rise to the occasion. You cannot do so—at least, not everybody can—when other people are laughing all the time.

I wonder, by the way, whether such things happen in these days?

There was a young man called McLean,
Who invented a fucking machine.
    Concave or convex,
    It would fit either sex,
And was perfectly simple to clean.

American.—Variants to last line:

The God-damndest thing ever seen . . .
And guaranteed used by the Queen . . .

I have puzzled till I can puzzle no more what the shape of this contrivance may have been, how it worked, and of what materials it was constructed. Out of American postal directories I obtained the addresses of 732 persons bearing the name of McLean, and circularized them, asking whether they are the lucky inventor, begging for further details, and offering to buy three or four dozen specimens for distribution among my friends.

Not a single reply up to date!

We may be sure that it was an efficient instrument, since the originator seems to have been of Scotch ancestry. It was "perfectly simple to clean": there you have the practical Scotsman.

P.S. The following letter on this subject has just reached me:

Williamstown, Mass.
2 March, 1928

Dear Sir,

Your circular of the 18 January addressed to my late husband has been opened by myself. I am sorry to have to inform you that he was not the maker of the instrument in question.

Pardon my frankness but, as you seem to be a man of the world, you will perhaps understand that, being now a widow, I am excusably interested in such a machine and would like, just for curiosity's sake, to purchase a specimen, if not too expensive. Should it be of a breakable nature, I might even take two. I will undertake to procure you a good many clients in our country, if the mechanism comes up to expectation.

Will you remember me when you have succeeded in discovering the inventor? Please try not to forget!

Yours gratefully in anticipation
Eleanor McLean

There was an old man of Brienz,
The length of whose cock was immense.
    With one swerve he could plug
    A boy's bottom in Zug
And a kitchen-maid's cunt in Coblenz.

A gargantuan implement in truth, seeing that the distance from Brienz to Zug is 58 kilometres, and to Coblenz immeasurably greater. If the author of this poem was not stretching a point, somebody else was plainly stretching a penis. The Swiss, for the rest, do not seem to be favoured in this respect (G. Westlake, F.R.S. *Penis-measurements in the Alps* London, 1889, plates V to XXI).

The nearest approach to such an object is what I have seen among the Masai, whose organs were also thrown on the screen many years ago during a lecture by Mrs. Sheldon to a select but delighted audience at the Zoological Society's rooms. The queer copulatory methods necessitated by such growths have been described with great detail by a number of Christian missionaries, who are keenly interested in such matters.

I should like to point out that the word "plug" does not rime with "Zug" except in Lancashire.

We may hazard a guess that the author of this poem was born at Accrington.

There was a young man of Calcutta,
Who tried to write "Cunt" on a shutter.
    He had got to "C-U-"
    When a pious Hindu
Knocked him arse over tip in the gutter.

These venerable lines are of interest to anthropologists; they emphasize a racial characteristic which we Europeans would do well to bear in mind. The Hindu did not behave in this brusque fashion because he was "pious"—"pious Hindu" is just a *façon de parler*—but because sex, to these people, is too solemn a thing to be joked about. Such is the Hindu's nature. His mind is a cesspool; his erotic literature must be read to be believed; but the idea of writing "cunt" on a shutter gives him the creeps.

They have forgotten how to laugh, these harassed and withered races.

There was an old man of Corfu,
Who fed upon cunt-juice and spew.
When he couldn't get this,
He fed upon piss —
And a bloody good substitute, too.

Variant:

When he couldn't get that,
He ate what he shat —
And bloody good shit he shat, too.

A horrid banquet; yet such perversions do occur. Coprophagous individuals are not unknown, and Prof. Maudsley writes (*Pathology of Mind,* p. 358) that "smell and taste are sometimes extremely vitiated . . . hair, filth, live frogs, worms and similar disgusting matters being swallowed with greedy relish."

As to drinking urine—the women of a tribe near Dodoma in Africa, whose name I forget, preserve a sample of their husband's urine during his absence from home, and drink it on his return. The custom is not popular among European ladies; not yet, at all events.

Corfu, nowadays, is remembered by tourists on account of a hideous building called the Achilleion. Edward Lear, the popularizer of limericks and doubtless the author of this very one, knew better and spent some of the happiest years of his life there. But the food is indifferent, and there is only one tavern in the town where drinkable wine can be procured.

There was a young lady of Kew,
Who said, as the curate withdrew:
"I prefer the dear vicar;
He's longer and thicker;
Besides, he comes quicker than you."

Kew is famous not for this or any other young lady
but for its botanic gardens, which prove what good
taste combined with perseverance and scientific knowledge can achieve under an English sky—with the assist-
ance of time. For they did not grow up in a day. The
Hortus Kewensis of William Alton was published as
early as 1789; its three volumes, consisting of some five
hundred pages each, are a catalogue of the plants already growing there. Caroline, wife of George II, spent
a great deal on the place; Sir William Chambers is responsible for some of the buildings; Cobbett, after run-
ning away from home, entered Kew as a gardener. When
one has lived, as I have, at 298 Kew Road (back room),
one has abundant opportunities of becoming acquainted
not only with its flora, but with attractive specimens of
its Sunday-afternoon fauna.

The last line of this poem shows the lady to have
been an ignorant little thing; she on page 31, I think,
would have clung to the curate despite his apparent de-
fects. Mere size cannot hope to compete with a rhythmic
ritardando con sentimento.

There was a young girl of Penzance,
Who boarded a bus in a trance.
    The passengers fucked her,
    Likewise the conductor;
The driver shot off in his pants.

This is the very episode which induced the City Fathers of Penzance to abolish those slow horse-buses in favour of quicker modes of public locomotion.

All too many cases are on record of girls and boys being abused while in a state of trance, or under the influence of anaesthetics or drugs; medical men themselves have not escaped the imputation of taking advantage of young patients on such occasions. One wonders, at the same time, how an event like this came to occur in England, in a public vehicle, and in broad daylight. How was it that none of these folk raised his voice in protest against the behaviour of the conductor and other passengers?

The driver alone seems to have preserved an outward air of decorum. The bus was presumably in motion, and he could not abandon the reins. One shudders to think what he would have done, had he been free to use his hands and move about like the others.

A deplorable business from beginning to end . . . . especially for the driver.

There was an old man of the Cape,
Who buggared a Barbary ape.
    Said the ape: "Sir, your prick
    Is too long and too thick,
And something is wrong with the shape."

Now what was wrong with the shape?

A variant to the last three lines will help to clear up the mystery:

    The ape said: "You fool!
    You've got a square tool;
You've buggared my arse out of shape."

This is a legitimate cause of remonstrance on the part of anybody in the ape's position. At the same time, I must say I have never seen a square tool, though many are not altogether round. Perhaps the ape was exaggerating. Perhaps it only *felt* square. "We generally find," says the Rev. Sydney Smith in his *Sketches of Moral Philosophy,* "that the triangular person has got into the square hole, the oblong into the triangular, and a square person has squeezed himself into the round hole."

According to Xavier Mayne (*The Intersexes,* N.D. p. 39; see also Garnier's well-known book) "entire genera of the ape and monkey family" are given to practising simili-sexual habits, "even when the male has access to the female for hetero-sexual copulation." This particular ape was obviously no novice at such diversions; indeed his language reveals him as a well-mannered but impenitent uranian.

Although to the best of my knowledge, no authentic case has yet come to light, it is a firmly established belief among African natives that the greater apes occasionally have intercourse with human beings. And why shouldn't they? It's all in the family . . . .

There was an old man of Stamboul
With a varicose vein in his tool.
  In attempting to come
  Up a little boy's bum
It burst, and he *did* look a fool.

Stamboul has been famous for these practices since long, the Sultans setting the example. The present government represses them, save in strictly religious circles. Whether there be any connexion between the two things I cannot say, but the Turks, in May of this year, struck me as a far more stupid race than they were before this repression began.

Varicose veins are a nuisance, and sometimes have to be treated surgically. Regarding the case in point, my medical expert writes: "Permanent venous dilatations of that particular organ are unknown in England, though the surrounding region is liable to such congestions (*e.g.* varicocele, haemorrhoids). It may be a Turkish variety of this complaint. To wear a tight worsted stocking round your member, as you do round your leg, does not commend itself to me, but perhaps Orientals approve of this treatment. These affected veins are often the result of pregnancy: can this apply to the present instance? I doubt it! You will see that the textbooks give 'prolonged standing' as another cause of the trouble, and I suspect it was the determining factor in the present case."

A certain amount of standing is no doubt desirable, but one can have too much of a good thing. "Prolonged standing" strikes me as the only adequate explanation of this accident. I think my expert deserves his fiver.

58

There was a young curate of Buckingham,
Who was blamed by the girls for not fucking 'em.
    He said: "Though my cock
    Is as hard as a rock,
Your cunts are too slack. Put a tuck in 'em."

    Some girls are hard to please. Here is another of these groundless complaints:

There was a young lady of Twickenham,
    Who regretted that men had no prick in 'em.
    On her knees every day
    To God she would pray
To lengthen, and strengthen, and thicken 'em.

    Perhaps the young man mentioned on page 32 would have suited her requirements; if not, then he on page 50.

    As to the curate of Buckingham—I regard his request as a reasonable one. I have been tempted to make it myself on several occasions.

There was an old Abbot of Khief,
Who thought the Impenitent Thief
Had bollocks of brass,
And an amethyst arse.
He died in this awful belief.

Variant to last two lines:

And an ivory arse —
A faith surpassing belief!

This poem bears the hall-mark of authenticity.

Khief, with the oldest cathedral in Russia, has always been famous as a holy city, and Russia itself has always been famous for the extravagances of its religious sects. No dogma so absurd, that some Russian will not be found to believe it. The modern Skoptzi, for instance, have nothing to learn from this old Abbot in point of gross superstition. It is consoling to know that he was regarded as a heretic, since his belief is described as "awful." *He died in this awful belief:* the pigheadedness of all sectarians!

The word "ivory" in the variant may refer to the product commercially called fossil ivory—the tusks of Siberian mammoths. But amethysts are also Russian stones, though I fancy that the finest specimens on the market (faintly clouded with brown) come from elsewhere. Had it not been a question of historical accuracy, the poet might with equal propriety have written "emerald" instead of "amethyst." Russian emeralds—discovered 1830—yield to none in point of tint, but they are even more liable to flaws than those from the old mines of Muso near Bogotá.

We may note that "Khief," as pronounced by Russians, does not rime with "thief."

It should.

There was a young girl of Baroda,
Who built a new kind of pagoda.
    The walls of its halls
    Were hung with the balls
And the tools of the fools that bestrode her.

A dainty little item from America.

The structure referred to must be of recent date. It is not mentioned in Fergusson's monumental work on Indian architecture, and nothing was known of it during my last stay in the old Mahratta city, else I should certainly have visited it in preference to cotton mills and other local sights. It must be a cosy kind of place.

Pagodas are expensive to build, and this young Amazon was doubtless rich; no richer, I daresay, than some of our English lady-millionaires. The late Baroness Burdett-Coutts, for instance, was famous for her munificence in endowing public buildings.

That temples should be used for the preservation of trophies is a universal trait. We need only think of St. George's Chapel or Westminster Abbey. Under the Greeks and Romans they served a similar purpose, besides being both banks and museums, and brothels.

There was a young girl who would make
Advances to snake after snake.
     She said: "I'm not vicious,
     But *so* superstitious!
I do it for Grandmama's sake."

This poem is obscure. Indeed, I should never have unravelled its meaning but for the fortunate discovery that the young lady in question was the granddaughter of Mrs. Ethel Bartlett of Nottingham.

Who remembers Mrs. Bartlett?

Yet she, together with Sir Francis Galton and others, was one of the pioneers of the eugenic cult in England; she wanted to "improve the race." This movement was at first considered something of a fad, and many of its supporters by their wild theories may well have deserved the name of faddists. Among these forgotten enthusiasts was Mrs. Bartlett. She is described as a sweet-natured old lady, but rather fanatical. The family still possesses a manuscript of hers which contains a furious denunciation of modern standards of health and intelligence—the result of faulty breeding, and of marriages which should never have been allowed. It goes on to review the parentage of some of the great men of antiquity, and finally asks: "Which of us women would not like to have Alexander of Macedon for a son?" This half-god among men, she declared, was the offspring of his mother Olympias and a serpent.

Such daring doctrines she must have inculcated into the mind of her granddaughter, and it is pathetic to note how the girl apologizes for appearing *vicious* and how, in describing herself as *superstitious,* she seems to waver between a reverence for the old lady's teaching and the reasonable conviction that unions like that of Olympias would prove sterile save in very exceptional cases.

She died at a ripe age, unmarried, on the 23 March, 1922.

There was an old man of Madrid,
Who cast loving eyes on a kid.
    He said: "Oh, my joy!
    I'll buggar that boy,
You see if I don't" — and he did.

Variant to last line:

And he out with his cock, and he did —

which, to my way of thinking, is a little gross.

Nothing venture, nothing win; moreover, to the pure all things are pure, and none but the brave deserve the fair. It takes a brave man to act like this in broad daylight ("you *see* if I don't": who can see at night-time?) and in a town like Madrid, where these practices do not seem to be prevalent. A recently published book, *The Quest* by Pio Baroja, deals largely with the poorer boys of Madrid, and contains not the least hint of such things. But this may prove nothing more than that the author was too decent-minded to give his young friends away.

Some Spanish kids are remarkably pretty, and have the most engaging manners—which they lose soon enough, together with their looks. The old man in the poem no doubt gave this particular one a few chocolates or a packet of cigarettes, or even both, and made an appointment for another meeting.

Who wouldn't?

There was a young fellow called Cary,
Who got fucking the Virgin Mary.
    And Christ was so bored
    At seeing Ma whored
That he set himself up as a fairy.

American; and it may be mentioned that "fairy" is the American term for a male prostitute.

This poem, with its faulty metre and irreverential suggestions, finds a place here only because, under the guise of an allegory, it hints at an important truth. Statistics are not available, but, from such first-hand knowledge as I have acquired in Paris and elsewhere, I should say that a great number of male prostitutes are children of harlots. The mother, fond as she may be of her son, cannot avoid initiating him at a tender age into all the mysteries of her trade; the temptation of eking out your own income with your boy's earnings is also hard to resist, and probably not worth resisting. A certain number of such youths become blackmailers; the rest, in due course, take to brothelkeeping and other more or less cheerful professions.

"Bored" is therefore not the right word; "excited" would be better. It is a case of mental over-stimulation backed by maternal encouragement.

There was an old girl of Silesia,
Who said: "As my cunt doesn't please yer,
    You might as well come
    Up my slimy old bum,
So Jimmy the tapeworm don't sieze yer."

We have all heard of prisoners, during their weary hours of captivity, making pets of mice and rats, and even spiders; but this is the only case that has come to my knowledge of a tapeworm becoming the object of human love, and bearing the homely name of "Jimmy."

I was so interested in these delightfully familiar relations between a worm and its Silesian host that I sent the verse to a scientific friend in Breslau for such observations as he might care to make. He forwarded my letter to an eminent surgeon and helminthologist, Dr. Brochowski of Cracow, whose reply, though not flattering to myself, shall be printed none the less:

"Dear Professor—, Thanks for yours of the 18 July with the query from your English correspondent. Having read some of his books in Polish translations, I took him to be a man of at least average intelligence. That cannot be the case, else the idea of making a pet of a tapeworm could never have occurred to him. Regarding the second part of his query, whether tapeworms ever bite, I can only say that I have performed hundreds of anal explorations with my finger, and have never been molested by them. There is a case on record, however, of a Dutch doctor being terribly mauled on one such occasion. I will look up the reference for you, and send it some time next week.

Yours very sincerely,
Ossip Brochowski."

There was a young lady named Skinner,
Who dreamt that her lover was in her.
    She woke with a start,
    And let a loud fart,
Which was followed by luncheon and dinner.

The muscular contraction provoked by a dream of this nature led to the same result as that described on page 37.

Note the truthfulness of the last line. The accident occurred at night, and if the poet had written "followed by dinner and luncheon" the meals would have been excreted in their wrong order—a feat which I defy anybody to perform.

The effects of these involuntary spasms are alluded to in another poem:

I dined with the Duchess of Lee,
Who asked: "Do you fart when you pee?"
    I said with some wit:
    "Do you belch when you shit?"
And felt it was one up to me.

A noble verse, and worthy of old England in its lack of polysyllables.

There was an old buggar of Como,
Who suddenly cried: "Ecce Homo!"
He tracked his man down
To the heart of the town,
And gobbled him off in the duomo.

Supplied by a well-known English man of letters, a summer visitor to the Italian lake district.

Pliny the Elder lived in Como and has now a hotel and a miserable street named after him; his nephew was born there, as was also Volta, who is indirectly responsible for the existence of telephones and other curses of humanity.

There is this to be said for the old man of Como, that he seems to have studied Latin in his youth, which is more than can be said of most of the inhabitants. They are hopelessly industrial; in other words, hopelessly dull.

The duomo or cathedral is described by Baedeker as one of the finest in North Italy. I enquired of the author why the old man should have selected just this structure for his purposes. He replied: "Idiot! Because it's safer than the Public Gardens."

We live and learn.

There was a young student of John's,
Who wanted to buggar the swans.
But the loyal hall-porter
Said: "Pray take my daughter!
The birds are reserved for the dons."

The loyalty of College-porters is traditional, and only surpassed by their politeness. Note the politeness of this one. It is typical of all of them.

The family of the *anatidae* seems to be favoured of mankind, and this much may be said in extenuation of the young man's proclivities that the swan is a comely bird. Not for nothing was it chosen by the Father of the Gods on a certain memorable occasion. If Zeus had transformed himself into a duck, Leda would hardly have succumbed to his charms.

Yet ducks are also attractive fowls, as any Chinaman will tell you. They have a veritable cult of them in that country, and that is why European residents refuse to eat them.

The last line may explain why the Thames swans are no longer served at banquets, as they were in the days of Queen Elizabeth. They are reserved for other, and perhaps worthier, purposes. Spanish geese are apt to be crotchety:

There was an old man of Santander,
Who attempted to buggar a gander.
But the silly old bird
Stuffed its arse with a turd —

We may be sure that English swans are more amenable to reason.

Said the venerable Dean of Saint Paul's
"Concerning them cracks in the walls —
       Do you think it would do,
       If we filled them with glue?"
The Bishop of Lincoln said: "Balls."

For the benefit of future generations it should be
said that not long ago certain ominous fissures appeared
in this edifice; they were attributed to ceaseless and heavy
traffic; experts were summoned, commissions appointed,
and costly repairs undertaken. An awkward discovery,
for no architect will admit that St. Paul's could be shaked
by motor-lorries unless, like certain other London
churches and English cathedrals in general, it were a
jerry-built affair.

This poem is open to grave suspicion. In the first
place, the Dean of St. Paul's is necessarily a gentleman,
and no gentleman says "them cracks." Secondly: what
was the Bishop of *Lincoln* doing there? Thirdly: the
expression attributed to His Lordship is too emphatic
to be consistent with good manners.

I regard the whole incident as apocryphal.

There was a young lady called Wylde,
Who kept herself quite undefiled
    By thinking of Jesus,
    Contagious diseases,
And the bother of having a child.

American.

This prudent young person hit upon the three chief deterrents to leading a loose life; a single one of them, I should have thought, would suffice for that purpose. The religious deterrent, once the strongest, seems to have lost something of its hold upon the modern woman. The second or medical one will never lose its hold; everybody knows that these diseases, a real menace to society, are now engaging the attention of public bodies all over Europe. Thirdly, the social stigma that would attach to a young girl, were she known to be pregnant, is incalculable—"bother" is a mild word for it—and often drives her into some nasty cottage down Cornwall way, or into the consulting room of people who "use instruments with a view to procuring a certain result"— the result to themselves being even more certain, namely, seven years.

There was a young man of Peru,
Who dreamt he was had by a Jew.
He woke up at night
In a hell of a fright,
And found it was perfectly true.

That dreams should convey premonitions of bodily states is well known to the medical profession. An on-coming illness is often heralded in dreams by a sense of uneasiness in that particular region of the body, and it is the experience of nearly all boys that nocturnal emissions are preceded by sexually suggestive visions on the part of the sleeper.

My Lima correspondent writes:

"From enquiries made among our Jewish colony I gather that sodomitic practices are quite as common among them as among Christians. There is this differ-ence, however, that the latter indulge in them from natural disposition; the Jews, because they consider them more hygienic and more economical than normal coition."

This little note, of great ethnological interest, is confirmed by the following:

There was a young Jew of Delray,
Who buggered his father one day.
He said: "I like rather
To stuff it up Father;
He's clean, and there's nothing to pay."

74

A thrifty youth, with strongly developed patriarchal instincts . . .

I detect a smack of incest in the above lines; readers of the Bible will not be surprised at such things.

Delray is in Michigan.

There was a young man of Madras,
Who was having a boy in the grass.
    Then a cobra-capello
    Said: "Hello, young fellow!"
And bit a piece out of his arse.

Late Victorian.

This is the second instance of a serpent speaking in the tongue of man, and quite as authentic as that recorded in Genesis.

Yet there is something wrong here. Cobras do not tear pieces of flesh out of their victims' bodies. As everybody knows, they inject poison: a poison so lethal that it is responsible for several thousand yearly deaths in India alone. Among the most famous researches into cobra-poison are the early ones of Sir Jos. Fayrer. They were conducted over a period of three years, and led him to the conclusion that antidotes such as aristolochia (proposed by Tennent and others) were of no avail. The treatment of snake-bite has made great strides since those days.

It is to be feared that the young man commemorated in this poem had no antidote at hand, and that he therefore paid with his life for what, in India, is a matter of individual taste.

There was a young lady of Louth,
Who returned from a trip in the South.
　　Her father said: "Nelly,
　　There's more in your belly
Than ever went in at your mouth."

An elegant example of the Golden Period.

My memories of Dundalk are confused; it rained all the time, and I recall nothing save a tavern where I spent several hours drinking the local brew (not bad) with a couple of decayed sailormen.

"Trip to the South" is vague. We may take it, none the less, that the girl left Ireland and went not exactly to the South Pole—else she would never have "returned"—but somewhere in that direction; moreover, that she was unaccompanied by her father. She went alone. Persons who travel alone are no longer children. She must have attained her majority, and girls of that age can do what they please and should not be subject to uncalled-for remarks on the part of anybody. The words uttered by the father will suffice to date this poem: it belongs to the Victorian era.

No modern parent will dream of addressing his grown-up daughter in such terms.

The girls who frequent picture-palaces
Set no store by psychoanalysis.
And though Mr. Freud
Is greatly annoyed,
They cling to their old-fashioned phalluses.

Query: "Old-fashioned *fallacies?*"
American; sophisticated school.

It struck me as so improbable that the gentleman in question should be annoyed at a trifle like this that I ventured to enquire in very civil terms of a disciple of his, likewise an expert, whether there was any truth in the suggestion. His answer ought to clear up the matter. He writes:

"Sir,

With reference to yours of the 3 instant, it is an impertinence to suppose that the Master should be annoyed, and I shall certainly not incommode Him with your nonsensical conundrum. Do you imagine that He, or anybody else, cares a fucking damn what the little bitches cling to? Let them cling to each other's twats, if they can.

Yours truly
(Dr.) E. Sauberger

P.S. By all means print this letter in any preposterous article or book you may be writing. E.S."

There was a young man of Kildare,
Who was having a girl in a chair.
　　At the sixty-third stroke
　　The furniture broke,
And his rifle went off in the air.

It was presumably one of those cheap Vienna
chairs which are exported in great quantities to Kildare
and other Irish towns, and which should never be used
for such purposes. But the young man was also to blame
for being so long about the business. Sixty-three strokes!
Even London chairs, excellent as they are, will feel that
strain.

People with such deliberate methods should stick
to the floor, where a rug, or preferably the fur of some
animal, will be found a welcome adjunct.

There was a young lady of Ealing,
Who had a peculiar feeling.
   She lay on her back,
   And opened her crack,
And pissed from the floor to the ceiling.

An Anonymous pamphlet lying before me (GEOG-
RAPHY WITHOUT GROANS: a Few Words on the Use
of Limericks in County Council Schools, London, 1913)
goes far to prove what I never thought possible—that
this verse-form has an educational value of its own.
The author, whom I take to be a schoolmaster and to
whom I wish all success, says that even a dry subject
like Geography can be made attractive to children; and
that if the place-names have some easily remembered
lines attached to them, the teacher's task is greatly facili-
tated, because at the mere mention of the verse "they
will at once brighten up, and give the correct latitude
and longitude, mountain-ranges, river-basins, exports,
and all information required." Especially is this the case,
he says, with those confusing London suburbs, a knowledge of which is so important to the poor children of
County Council Schools.

MASTER (sternly): What, don't you boys know
anything about Ealing? Haven't I taught you that

There was a young lady of Ealing,
Who had a peculiar —

CHORUS: Oh, yessir! She piddled all over the
ceiling. It's the birth-place of Huxley, and exports City

clerks, and imports dirty washing, and is watered by three main drains, and lies in latitude—

MASTER: That will do.

There was a young man of Loch Leven,
Who went for a walk about seven.
    He fell into a pit
    That was brimful of shit,
And now the poor buggar's in heaven.

This faulty rime must have been concocted by an Englishman or American; no native of the country would think of making "Loch Leven" go together with "Heaven," save so far as natural scenery is concerned. And the accident becomes intelligible if we suppose that it occurred not in the morning but at seven in the evening. At that hour of an autumn or winter month it is already pitch-dark in the latitude of Loch Leven.

The *shit-pits,* as they are locally called, used to be very common in England. Fabyan's Chronicles (1516) relate that in 1252 a Jew of Tewkesbury fell into one of them on a Saturday, but refused to be taken out on his Sabbath; whereupon the Earl of Gloucester, who was not to be outdone in religious zeal, refused to take him out on Sunday. On Monday he was found to be dead. They were introduced into Scotland about 150 years ago by one James Macpherson, a tea-merchant and shrewd pioneer, who had observed them in China, where they are known as *pupu-holes.* To disappear into an unfenced *pupu-hole*—if fenced round, how are you going to use it?—is an ordinary form of death out there, and even in Scotland fatal accidents have lately become so frequent that the custom, despite its obvious conveniences, is beginning to lose ground.

As to the victim being now in Heaven—we must take our poet's word for that. I think, unless they have fished him out, he will be found where he was.

Thus spake I AM THAT I AM:
"For the Virgin I don't give a damn.
    What pleases me most
    Is to buggar the Ghost,
And then be sucked off by the Lamb."

This lyric savours of profanity, and yet its author-ship has been claimed by no less than eleven Bishops and five minor Canons of the Church of England. I am not going to print all their names, much less shall I un-dertake the invidious task of deciding which of them is the real author; that would stir up a veritable wasps' nest. All I venture to suggest is that a gentleman en-dowed with poetic talents of this nature would have done well to seek employment in some other walk of life.

The lines are obviously derived from the immortal trilogy:

Thus spake the King of Siam:
"For women I don't care a damn.
    But a fat-bottomed boy
    Is my pride and my joy —
They call me a buggar: I am."

which is followed by:

Then up spake the Bey of Algiers:
"I am old and well stricken in years,
    And my language is blunt;

But a cunt *is* a cunt,
And fucking *is* fucking" — (*loud cheers*).

which calls for:

Then up spake the young King of Spain:
"To fuck and to buggar is pain.
　　But it's not *infra dig*
　　On occasion to frig,
And I do it again and again."

There was a young man of Cape Horn
Who wished he had never been born.
And he wouldn't have been
If his father had seen
That the end of the rubber was torn.

I should apologise for inserting this well-known lyric but for the fact that so perfect a specimen of the Golden Period cannot be excluded from a collection like this. The smoothness of the versification: the glamour that hangs about mysterious regions like Tierra del Fuego: the wistfulness of the opening lines and the anticlimax of the last one—they all testify to the genius of the Unknown Poet.

It is not surprising that the young man in question should have suffered from melancholia. Travellers concur in stating that this is one of the gloomiest landscapes on earth; a desolation of fog, drizzle, and snow. Charles Darwin, in his *Voyage of the Beagle,* tells us that "Death, instead of Life, seems the predominant spirit" of those parts, and a more recent writer, Metcalfe, reports that the natives are letting themselves die out, apparently, from "sheer weariness of living."

I cannot say how that rubber came to reach Cape Horn; maybe it was bartered by the mate of a passing whaler for a dozen sea-otter skins. These appliances are supposed to be of French origin, but they must have been already known at the Byzantine Court, if what Gibbon calls "the most detestable precautions" of Theodora were of this kind. And some curious material has now come to light (Prof. O. Schwanzerl, *Kondonsgebrauch im frü-*

hesten Mittelalter, Budapesth, 1903) showing that they were in use under the Merovingians. They were made of deerskin—*gegerbtes Hirschleder*—and smeared with tallow—*Unschlick*—to facilitate penetration. (For an analogous use of leather *see* Mime VI and VII of Herodas). The invention was attributed to the Queen who, while fond of lovers, insisted, and rightly, on the legitimacy of her offspring.

The world would be a better place, if modern women had the same respect for their husbands.

GEOGRAPHICAL INDEX